First Facts™

Water All Around

Saving Water

by Rebecca Olien

Consultant:
Peter R. Jaffé, Professor
Department of Civil and Environmental Engineering
Princeton University
Princeton, New Jersey

Capstone
press
Mankato, Minnesota

First Facts is published by Capstone Press,
151 Good Counsel Drive, P.O. Box 669, Mankato, Minnesota 56002.
www.capstonepress.com

Library of Congress Cataloging-in-Publication Data
Olien, Rebecca.
    Saving water / by Rebecca Olien.
    p. cm.—(First facts. Water all around)
    Includes bibliographical references and index.
    ISBN 0-7368-3699-3 (hardcover)
    1. Water conservation—Juvenile literature. I. Title. II. Series.
TD388.O95 2005
333.91'16—dc22   2004011979

Summary: Describes the sources of freshwater on the earth and ways people can conserve water.

Editorial Credits
Christine Peterson, editor; Linda Clavel, designer; Kelly Garvin, photo researcher;
    Scott Thoms, photo editor

Photo Credits
Bruce Coleman Inc./Norman Owen Tomalin, 7
Corbis/Ariel Skelley, 16; Brownie Harris, 17; David Lees, 10; Pete Saloutes, 5; Royalty Free, 6;
    Roy Morsch, cover; Steve Prezant, 11; Yann Arthus-Bertrand, 20
Creatas, 18–19
Index Stock Imagery/Dr. Eric Chalker, 9; Grantpix, 14–15
Photodisc, 12, 13

1 2 3 4 5 6 10 09 08 07 06 05

Table of Contents

Everyone Shares Water

All living things share the earth's water. People, plants, and animals need water to live. Each day, more people are born who need the earth's water. But only a small amount of the earth's water is safe for people to use. People need to save water by using less.

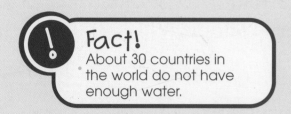

Fact!
About 30 countries in the world do not have enough water.

Freshwater

Most people believe there is plenty of water. **Salt water** in oceans makes up 97 percent of the earth's water. People can't drink salt water.

Only 3 percent of the earth's water is **freshwater**. Most freshwater is frozen in **glaciers**. People have to use freshwater from lakes, rivers, and **aquifers**.

Laws Protect Water

Governments pass laws to save water. Some laws **protect** freshwater sources. Others keep water clean. Some states and cities have laws to **limit** when people can water lawns and gardens.

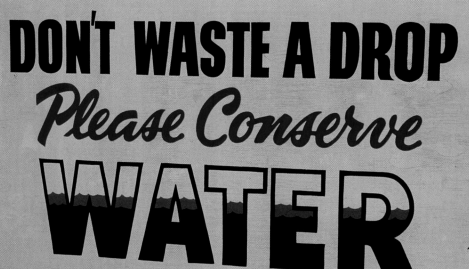

DON'T WASTE A DROP
Please Conserve
WATER

SAN SIMEON ACRES COMMUNITY SERVICE DISTRICT

9

Businesses Save Water

Businesses use millions of gallons (liters) of water. Factories use water to make paper and cars. Power plants use water to make electricity.

Many businesses save water by reusing it. Car washes save soapy water in underground tanks. The water is reused to wash other cars.

Saving Water Outdoors

Farmers use water to grow crops. To save water, some farmers grow crops that need less water. Other farmers reuse city water on crops.

At home, people use the most water outdoors. To save water, people should only water lawns when needed. Using sprinklers at dusk also saves water.

Cities Save Water

Cities save water in many ways. Cities collect water that washes into the **sewers**. Cities clean the water and send it to factories. City workers also reuse water to clean streets and water plants in parks.

Fun Fact!
It takes 39,090 gallons (147,972 liters) of water to make a new car.

Saving Water at Home

People can save water at home. To save water, turn off the faucet when brushing your teeth. Take shorter showers.

People can save water at home in other ways. Buy toilets that use less water. Run clothes washers only when they are full.

Saving Water

Saving water makes sure all living things have freshwater to drink. People, plants, and animals share the same freshwater. Everyone must work together to save water and keep it clean.

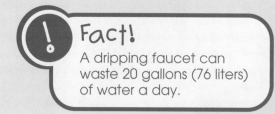

! Fact!
A dripping faucet can waste 20 gallons (76 liters) of water a day.

How would you like a cold glass of ocean water? Scientists can remove the salt from ocean water. Ocean water is heated or pushed through a filter to remove the salt. People can drink the water once the salt is removed.

Hands On: Removing Salt

Scientists heat ocean water to remove the salt. Try this experiment to see how hot salt water can become freshwater.

What You Need

2 teaspoons (30 mL) salt
clean jar with lid
hot water

What You Do

1. Place the salt in the jar.
2. Fill the jar half full with hot water from the faucet.
3. Cover the jar with the lid.
4. Wait 10 minutes.
5. Notice the drops of water forming on the sides and lid of the jar. Carefully remove the lid. Taste the drops on the inside of the lid. Do they taste salty? The water on the lid is evaporated fresh water. The salt stays behind in the jar.

Glossary

aquifer (AK-wuh-fuhr)—an underground lake

freshwater (FRESH-wa-tur)—water that has little or no salt; most ponds, rivers, lakes, and streams have freshwater.

glacier (GLAY-shur)—a large sheet of frozen freshwater; glaciers are found in mountains and polar areas.

limit (LIM-it)—to keep within a certain amount; laws help save water by limiting how much people can use.

protect (pruh-TECT)—to keep safe

salt water (SAWLT WAH-tur)—water that is salty; salt water is found in oceans.

sewer (SOO-ur)—an underground pipe that carries away waste water

Read More

Dalgleish, Sharon. *Saving Water.* Our World, Our Future. Philadelphia: Chelsea House, 2003.

Nelson, Robin. *We Use Water.* First Step Nonfiction. Minneapolis: Lerner, 2003.

Internet Sites

FactHound offers a safe, fun way to find Internet sites related to this book. All of the sites on FactHound have been researched by our staff.

Here's how:
1. Visit *www.facthound.com*
2. Type in this special code **0736836993** for age-appropriate sites. Or enter a search word related to this book for a more general search.
3. Click on the **Fetch It** button.

FactHound will fetch the best sites for you!

Index